Lord, Did I Really Shave My Legs For This?

Lisa Mills

W0009564

INFINITY
PUBLISHING

Copyright © 2013 by Lisa Mills

ISBN 978-0-7414-8380-5

Scripture references that are noted have been taken from the New International Version Bible. Most scripture thoughts, ideas, or meanings have been simplified, paraphrased, or abbreviated through the author's own words and interpretation. The complete scriptural reference can be located in the King James Version of the Bible. The ideas, concepts, and advice presented in this book are biblically based from one person's life experiences and perception. For any unresolved related issues in your own life, always seek the advice of a minister, pastor, counselor, or therapist.

Credits:
Cover Design by Michael Pippin, www.levelsevengraphics.com
Photography by Amber Phinisee, www.amberphiniseephotography.com

Printed in the United States of America

Published May 2013

INFINITY PUBLISHING
1094 New DeHaven Street, Suite 100
West Conshohocken, PA 19428-2713
Toll-free (877) BUY BOOK
Local Phone (610) 941-9999
Fax (610) 941-9959
Info@buybooksontheweb.com
www.buybooksontheweb.com

Contents

Foreword i

Dedication... iii

Introduction...v

1. Procrastination 1

2. Endurance 3

3. Listening..5

4. Pride..7

5. Conflict.. 9

6. Fasting 11

7. Hospitality... 13

8. Maturity 15

9. Order.. 17

10. Correction.. 19

11. Provision.. 21

12. Honesty.. 23

13. Heaven... 25

14. Trust 27

15. Kindness 29

16. Parenting.. 31

17. Appearance 33

18. Prosperity... 35

19. Aging 37

20. Marriage 39

21. Criticism 41

22. Rest 43

23. Home 45

24. Expectation 47

25. Patience 49

26. Overcoming 51

27. Prayer 53

28. Love 55

29. Wisdom 57

30. Laughter 59

31. Purpose 61

Testimonial 63

Reflection 67

Acknowledgements 69

Information 73

Foreword

"Lord, did I really shave my legs for this?" is a daily dose of laughter laced with lessons for living. As wives, mothers, women, we are in continual motion, both naturally and spiritually. Our days are rigorous and it's a constant juggle to make sure every physical, emotional, and material need of our families is met. Yet, somehow, in the midst of routine and the daily grind of life's natural demands, our own spirits are forever crying out for renewal.

Lisa's devotional is a tightly woven blend of lighthearted humor mixed with the realness of life. Both are knitted together so intricately throughout this book that you won't even realize your spirit has been fed what it was lacking until you stop laughing. If I know anything about Lisa, it's that she has learned many of her spiritual lessons through laughter. She teaches us in the same unique manner as she has learned in her own world; through witty events which parallel with the seriousness of life. She knows the shortest route to a heavy heart is straight through the funny bone. It's her greatest desire to touch both at the same time. Listen to her voice and you are sure to see His face.

I am so excited to present to you the funniest, most practical and applicable daily devotional I, personally, have ever read. You'll get a good laugh, a spiritual insight, and a challenge to grow. This is *definitely* worth shaving your legs for!

-Denise Smith

Author of *Seeds of Purpose*

Dedication

I would like to dedicate this book to my mother, JoAnn Bussell, and my sister, Angela Ayers, two of the "realest" women whom I have ever known. [Realest: An adjective that is sometimes used to describe a Southern woman who displays uninterrupted loyalty, possesses unwavering love, and shares uninhibited opinions, all while frequently going barefoot, even outdoors.]

Mom, I just want you to know that every time you sent me out to the porch for a few minutes, right before bedtime to get all my giggles out, I could still hear you laughing on the other side of the door. That porch was my first stage and you were my first fan. Thank you. What you have sacrificed and given to my life is priceless. Thank you for knowing there was more in me than even I knew. I am proud that you are my mom. I love you more than you could possibly imagine!

And to my very first best friend, my sister and my giggle partner-in-crime out on that porch; making you laugh is like putting on a pair of old skinny jeans and finding money in the pocket! I love you more than any amount of words on a page could convey. Without your support, my life would look so much different today. You have loved me at my worst and celebrated me at my best. I am forever grateful for your love!

Introduction

There is nothing that irritates me more than shaving my legs for no reason. The mere fact that I have shaved indicates that I have some expectation of a benefit from all the effort that goes into this particular feminine chore. Seriously, don't let me happen to shave then we have some sort of unseasonable cold front that moves in and I ended up wearing pants for the whole "prickle free" period! What?! I didn't even get credit. No one had a chance to see!

I mean, I don't mind shaving if I am going on vacation to the beach and everyone will notice if I don't, or I attend a wedding where (Lord, forbid) I am forced to wear a skirt, or even if I have to wear Capri pants to go grocery shopping, because all of my jeans are in the laundry. (Okay, actually in that last instance, I would probably still only shave the part of my legs that someone may see. So I'm not sure if that one really even counts.) But to just spend the effort of actually bending all the way over to remove hair from the entire lower half of my body, when no one will likely see it? Well, I just can not promote that sort of madness.

I know several women who are, in my opinion, addicted to shaving. If there is the slightest stubble, out comes the razor and they are smooth as silk in less than ten minutes. And just between you and me, I have a cousin who, I swear, keeps her razor in a holster on her side! Seriously, who has that kind of expectation in life? What could you possibly be preparing for besides going into labor and having your clean shaven legs photographed beautifully in a set of stirrups? I see absolutely no need to do this sort of time consuming, female ritual more than once every seven to ten business days. Unless of course it is winter, in which case you can take all the time you need until spring.

I am sure that all of this speaks volumes about me. And since we are sharing, you should probably know that I have actually pondered the above train of thought long enough that I now relate it to many things in my life. Of course, they are all annoying things, but so is having to shave. Whether standing in between two arguing teenage sons, or being the only woman to show up at a potluck dinner with a bag of Oreos, or watching a movie with my husband only to hear him start snoring halfway through the opening credits...well, each one of these moments beg me to take a deep breath and look toward heaven while asking, "Lord, did I really shave my legs for this?"

There is something very effective about asking that question aloud that enables me to take a small, mental break and then regroup with a determination to not sweat the little things - oh, and to not punch things. Definitely, do not punch things.

Actually, this question will often remind me to be grateful that I have any of those things to deal with at all. Dealing with them means that I am above ground, and I must admit, that is a plus! Life is short. Too short to worry or fret over stuff that just simply does not matter in the big scheme of things. I have learned that enjoying a moment is a choice. Not allowing a less-than-stellar moment effect you is also a choice. So the next time that you find yourself debating whether or not to egg your neighbor's car in the middle of the night because they continuously allow their dogs to romp all over your lawn, just remember, you have a choice to control your emotions. Well, that and the fact that running around, throwing anything sounds like doing cardio. Oh yeah, and also, the price of eggs has really gone up this year. So, anyway, all I'm saying is, just choose wisely.

<u>Day 1</u>

Yesterday, I may or may not have restarted the dryer in order to avoid folding the laundry...twice!

Procrastination

Proverbs 13:4 *(NIV) - A sluggard's appetite is never filled, but the desires of the diligent are fully satisfied.*

Occasionally, I fall into the trap of procrastination. It is something that I battled for many years and now have to be vigilant about when I feel it creeping back up. I have noticed that it first begins with the small things, like not folding a load of laundry, not opening the day's mail, or even waiting to schedule a hair appointment. Before you know it, you are secretly sitting through a parent teacher conference in your husband's underwear because you have no idea where a clean pair of your own would be, your water is disconnected while you're bathing the dog because you did not pay the bill, and you still have to give this week's office presentation looking like Julia Childs instead of Julia Roberts because your hairdresser is all booked up!

God wants us to be diligent in our pursuit of all things. Diligent means having or showing care and conscientiousness in one's work or duties. I know that when I allow procrastination to steal my "care" it ends up stealing with it my order, my time and ultimately my peace. You can't even give it an inch. It will absolutely take miles from you!

Today, decide to be diligent about your responsibilities. Set your mind now that nothing will allow you to put off until tomorrow what can be accomplished (and blessed) today. Having said that, I think that I may have some laundry to fold!

Day 2

Well, if I had a dollar for every mile I had ever run, I would have fifty cents.

Endurance

Galatians 6:9 *(NIV) - Let us not become weary in doing good, for at the proper time we will reap a harvest if we do not give up.*

This year I have really been waging war on my non-healthy habits. I am determined to get fit and lead a healthier lifestyle, even if it kills me. And believe me, there are days that I feel like it will! When you are as out of shape as I am, working out can shock your joints and muscles in ways that you can not imagine. If that wasn't reason enough to quit, you can always count on those closest to you for unsolicited feedback. Just the other day I was out walking in my neighborhood with my sons when we began to smell a faint whiff of smoke. I wondered aloud where it might be coming from, only to here my oldest son reply, "Oh, I just assumed it was coming from your knees." There really are days when I fully understand why some animals eat their young.

Beginning something that is difficult is never easy and seeing it through to the end is even harder at times. I know that there have been moments in my life that I felt like I would never see something to its end or that whatever I was going through would surely consume me by the time it was all over. Having lived a little while and long enough to have instances where I had to dig deeper and push through, I have learned to have a made up mind to outlast my situation. During each one of these instances, I thought I would surely lose out because of my wanting to quit. It has taken me a few years to realize that at some point everyone wants to quit, but if we push past that and keep going no matter the difficulty, we will see that is where the winning happens!

Is there something pressing in your life today that feels bigger than what you can handle? I promise that if you are faithful to endure, see it all the way through to the end, there will be victory waiting for you. Ask God to help you, strengthen you, and remind you that there is a harvest for all that you are sowing right now!

Day 3

I can hear one of my sons singing in the shower at the top of his lungs. That or either he is removing them one at a time, I can't tell.

Listening

James 1:19 *(NIV) - My dear brothers and sisters, take note of this: Everyone should be quick to listen, slow to speak and slow to become angry.*

I would like to thank the woman walking ahead of me today at the health department for not turning around and making eye contact with me when my youngest son asked, "Mom is this where you got me pregnant?" However, when I responded, "No honey, don't be silly...that was at the hospital", she could've saved the giggling for later. I have really got to pay better attention to that kid when he is talking and my mind is somewhere else!

There is a reason that God instructs us to be quick to listen. If you reflect back on any misunderstandings that you have experienced with others, you could probably credit someone with NOT listening to at least half of those incidents. When we do not listen, which means to give one's attention to a sound, we choose to only access a portion of what is being released and therefore we do not have complete information. Most people hear but very few listen. This is because hearing is done with your ears...listening is done with your attention.

Make a commitment to become a better listener, to be fully attentive to what others are saying. Since we know that what we give is what we get, if we become better listeners, we are bound to have others attention when it is our time to speak.

Day 4

Being embarrassed is a feeling of no control and helplessness. Both of which I find makes me want to set my hair on fire rather than feel either of these two things.

Pride

Proverbs 16:18 *(NIV) – Pride goes before destruction, a haughty spirit before a fall.*

A few years ago I attended a grant writing workshop. During the "around the room" style introductions, I learned that I had more working knowledge of the subject than most of the other attendees whose education exceeded mine. I remember sitting there feeling quite proud of myself. I got to enjoy that feeling for one entire day of what was a two-day workshop. On the morning of the next session, I arrived early to mingle with the other attendees over coffee. When I got up from my chair to head toward the breakfast table for another doughnut (also known as my kryptonite) I stepped wrong and fell flat on my face. I was wearing dress clothes that tend to give you a more propelled trajectory across a waxed tile floor when momentum is on their side. (By the way, I have a lot of "momentum".) I did a beautiful, slip-n-slide move for at least fifteen feet and right into a table with plenty of chairs. My head and arms went first, with my feet and legs flying so high that I thought they would arch all the way over to touch my head. When it was all said and done, let's just say that I have seen Christmas lights that were not that tangled!

We are never less like Christ than when we put ourselves above others. His desire for us is to view others as He sees them; people of great worth and immeasurable value! Many times it is our own insecurities that cause us to be prideful. Solomon warns us in scripture about the end result of allowing these feelings to rule our lives.

Make up your mind today that you will choose to see others as equally loved and valued brothers and sisters in Christ. After all, I would hate for you to "blow out a hoof on the way to the trough" in order for God to get your attention!

Day 5

I think most men would rather run with scissors than answer their wife's questions about how she looks in a pair of jeans.

Conflict

Romans 12:18 *(NIV) - If it is possible, as far as it depends on you, live at peace with everyone.*

Sitting in my car facing another vehicle as we are both waiting on the same car to leave the coveted front row parking space at Wal-Mart. This, my friends, is known as the equivalent of a third grade "staring contest." Realizing that the other car had no intention of moving along to another space, I had no choice but to up the ante and put on my turn signal, indicating the equivalent of the "I double dog dare you!"

Most people do not enjoy conflict. While there are certainly times that conflict is unavoidable, I believe that we are too quick to enter into it over the silliest of things. Most of the time it is in order to prove our own pride or superiority in a situation. God knew that it would not be possible for us to avoid conflict altogether; however, He challenges us to examine our heart's responsibility when faced with it. We are to do what is in our own power to avoid conflict if we can. We are not to depend solely on others to make a responsible choice toward peace but, instead, do all that we can in order to be at peace with others.

Determine now in your heart that the next time that you are faced with conflict that you will do all that is necessary to control your emotions, to align your heart with God's word, and to provide peace where it is absent.

<u>Day 6</u>

Dear Fellow Praisers,

If you are fasting, please know that it is perfectly acceptable to carry around toothpaste if you happen to be out of mints. Butterscotch does not work.

Sincerely,
Everyone on Your Pew

Fasting

Isaiah 58:6 *(NIV) - Is not this the kind of fasting I have chosen: to loose the chains of injustice and untie the cords of the yoke, to set the oppressed free and break every yoke?*

A few years ago my family was in the middle of a Daniel fast when we were invited to a birthday party. Knowing that the Daniel Fast would not allow us to eat meat or sweets, I knew this would be a little tricky. But it was also a relative's birthday and we would really need to make an appearance. We made it all the way through the entire party without one problem, until we began to leave. I remember trying to round up my youngest son from all the party goers, only to find him sitting on a bench with a few other boys who had apparently been passing little pieces of cake down the line for my son to enjoy. When I asked him to explain, he said, "Don't worry mom, God's not mad. I scrapped all the icing off first!"

There are times when I feel like I need to cut out distractions and really focus on a matter. It is during these times that I find fasting is my greatest tool. No matter what I am giving up or for how long, it refocuses me and channels my faith in a way like nothing else can. I have seen some of the greatest breakthroughs in my life come by way of fasting.

If you are not familiar with it, I challenge you to do a little study on fasting. There are many different forms and perspectives. However, one thing remains the same; it works!

<u>Day 7</u>

I wonder if there was even just one pilgrim woman who all of the other pilgrim women looked over at before the big feast and said, "Oh honey, how 'bout you just bring the plates?"

Hospitality

1st Peter 4:9 (NIV) - Offer hospitality to one another without grumbling.

I am surrounded by women who can cook, decorate and craft like no one else! Unfortunately, these are not ANY of my gifts. I appreciate these gifts in other women and am actually content to not possess them myself. (I once sewed a pair of shorts in home economics that looked more like one half of a girdle and the other half of a skirt. I called it the "skirdle." Patent still pending.) However, I do enjoy showing love to others through acts of kindness. Therefore, one year I offered to host Thanksgiving dinner at my house so that my sister could just show up, enjoy the holiday with everyone, and not have to slave for days making her annual feast for our entire family. I would like to tell you that God smiled on me and that I hosted a holiday dinner that would make even Paula Deen weep with gratitude, but we both know that is not where this story is headed. The only thing I clearly remember is opening the door to my wall oven to baste the turkey when a back draft of fire shot up the wall and across my kitchen ceiling. I ran out of my house screaming for my husband and dialing my sister's phone number at the same time. My husband managed to get the turkey under control just as my sister came squealing tires into my driveway. She emerged from her car half dressed with wet hair and a skinned up knee which she acquired from frantically running to her car when I called. The only thing I could think to say was, "Don't worry, I saved the yams!" Hmmm, it's weird, but since then I have noticed that my sister really prefers the kind of hospitality that comes in the form of a greeting card.

Hospitality is no more than serving others generously with warmth and kindness. Serving others in this way is when we most resemble Christ!

Vow to show hospitality to someone today and watch as God miraculously allows the act of serving others to richly bless your own life!

Day 8

Well, this new TIME magazine cover of a three year-old-child, standing flat-footed on a chair in order to breastfeed from his mother, seems inappropriate. I mean seriously, who lets kids that age stand on furniture?

Maturity

1 Corinthians 13:11 *(NIV) - When I was a child, I talked like a child, I thought like a child, I reasoned like a child. When I became a man, I put the ways of childhood behind me.*

It's easy for me to remember the almost five-year age difference between my two children, but I can sometimes easily forget an age difference between myself and another woman. For instance, at one time I worked in an office with several other women and a few of them were considerably younger than me. Since most of our conversations centered on work-related topics, our age difference rarely mattered. However, one afternoon I returned from lunch to find a coworker, who was barely twenty years old, asking for a legal pad in order to record some notes. Pointing to a nearby desk monitor, I asked her why she didn't just write them on the computer. She replied, "Are you serious? That would be defacing company property, Mrs. Lisa!" Instead of explaining what I meant, I simply said, "Yes, you are right. I'm sure it's just a sugar-high. I must have had too much dessert at lunch."

We are all guilty of not acting our age or being silly at one time or another. There is absolutely nothing wrong with being silly in the moment or misunderstanding the meaning of something (like the above scenario). However, when your life is constantly lived at an immature level, you can never expect to walk in all that God has for your life. Our lives, minds, and relationships were meant to increase; not just in length but also in depth. Some of the greatest moments of our lives will be those of development, revelation, and insight. If we are not continuously growing to reach our next level these moments are sure to pass us by.

Make up your mind today that you will enjoy each moment of your life at every level. And that you will also continuously live in search of growth, so that you may discover all that was intended for your life to become its fullest. Maturity is not your age. It is your mindset!

<u>*Day 9*</u>

For the life of me, I can not understand why anyone would have a need for scented toilet paper, yet purchase unscented antiperspirant.

Order

I Corinthians 14:33 (NIV) - But everything should be done in a fitting and orderly way.

I recently had a yearly physical exam. I am unlike the majority of women who would rather be shot than have this done. It is a necessary, annual event in my life. I don't usually spend much time fretting about this appointment; however, this particular day during the usual quick prep before leaving the house, I noticed that I was in serious need of a pedicure. With no time to apply polish, I hurried to get to my appointment. After arriving and signing in, I made my way back to the exam room where I instantly spotted a way out of any toenail polish embarrassment that I might have had. I couldn't believe my luck. Lying right on the counter were a pair of complimentary disposable socks. I hadn't remembered ever getting them before but never the less, I changed into my paper wardrobe and waited for the nurse. As she entered the room, a confused look immediately came across her face. "I'm so sorry, Mrs. Mills. I was in the middle of prepping this room and left some little slip covers for the stirrups lying out but now I can't seem to find them. Hold on. I will go get another set." I should mention here that it is very tricky to sit Indian style while wearing a paper gown, in order to hide your feet and any stolen merchandise that may accompany them.

I realize that sometimes it can be difficult to do things the right way, but more times than not, we simply choose to do what we want, when we want, and with no regard at all for order. We act on impulse or out of emotion because it is easiest. It's when we choose to react rather than respond, that we most likely end up in a mess. It takes restraint and also respect to act within the perimeters of rules.

God instructs us to do all things in an orderly way. Order has its place and exists for a reason, namely for your and my benefit! God only instructs us in ways that are meant to prosper our lives. If this is an area of struggle for you, ask the Lord to lead your decisions and actions. If order is what you truly desire, order is what you will find.

<u>Day 10</u>

In the middle of watching a television show about playground bullying, my son exclaims, "It is not cool to embarrass people, mom. I mean, no one likes to be mutilated!" I replied, "I think you mean, humiliated. But you are correct either way."

Correction

Proverbs 15:31 *(NIV) - Whoever heeds life-giving correction will be at home among the wise.*

Be very, very patient when your husband uses the word "may" and isn't referring to a calendar month. It will usually be followed by his honesty that is not so cleverly disguised by his tact. For instance, my husband and I really enjoy going for a drive together. As parents of two teenagers, it is one of our few getaway moments. While recently enjoying one of these drives, out of the blue and with a wrinkled-up nose he asks me, "Honey, *may* I ask if you have recently changed lotions or perfumes?" After staring straight ahead and counting to ten, I said, "No." He responded, "No, you haven't changed lotions or perfumes?" I replied, "No. I meant, you *may not* ask me that."

Correction can be a tricky thing to give and sometimes an even trickier thing to receive. I have found that some of the greatest moments in my life have been produced from some of the hardest corrections I have had to receive. Our flesh never enjoys correction, but if our hearts are aligned with the word of God and we are determined to overcome any offense that may try to steal the value of the correction, our lives will flourish immensely.

Make a decision to change your perspective regarding correction. Determine that you will not view it as a negative thing, but instead more like a navigation system that keeps you on the road and headed in the right direction!

Day 11

I'm thinking that when Thelma and Louise ran away, they weren't paying $3.93 a gallon for gas!

Provision

Psalm 111:5 *(NIV)* - *He provides food for those who fear him; he remembers his covenant forever.*

As I was practically skipping to the register at a local store tonight, I realized that couponing makes me more excited about the price of toilet paper than any one woman probably should ever be. In light of the downward turn of our economy, I have found several ways to trim our budget. One that has really helped is using coupons. I have been networking with other moms and their family budgets and have found coupons to now be the preferred drug of Middle American women. I have never seen them so elated and giddy, over things like forty-seven bottles of mustard, eighteen cases of cat food and as many tubes of toothpaste as a second hand Subaru can haul, all for $2.97 plus tax. And I must admit, now that I have given it a try, I may need Betty Ford herself to help me stop!

God promises in His word that He will continually take care of all of our needs. He is not moved by anything except our faith concerning these promises. He is so pleased when you and I determine to trust Him for all that we need just as we would a natural father. He loves us and wants nothing more than to take care and provide for His children.

Despite what your personal budget may reflect, or what the latest national report on our economy may project, or even what your friends and family may be saying about their own finances, determine today that you will continue to trust the One who owns it all.

Hmmm, now if I could just score some gasoline coupons, I would be the Donald Trump of my neighborhood.

Day 12

Direct deposit: (noun) A plan to transfer an employee's salary directly to the employee's account. It is Latin for the ability to call in sick on Friday.

Honesty

Proverbs 12:19 *(NIV) - Truthful lips endure forever, but a lying tongue lasts only a moment.*

The other night, my youngest son asked to show me a card trick. "Mom, pick a card from this deck", he instructed. I picked a card from the deck and held it close to my chest so that only I could see what it revealed. He then announces that he can magically guess exactly which card I am holding. Then he proceeds to actually guess...fifty-one times! Afterwards, I explained that maybe this should be called a "game" and that I am not sure he should call this a card "trick" if it takes fifty-one guesses for him to reveal the correct card. He replied, "Well, it wouldn't have taken that long if you would have just said that I guessed correctly a lot sooner." My son, the honest magician, ladies and gentleman!

It isn't always easy to be honest. Sometimes it is just a matter of perspective that trips us up. Many times we justify our thinking with excuses and reasoning. However, it isn't the words you choose but the intention to deceive that makes one dishonest. I have learned that dishonesty is not a vocabulary issue, it is a heart issue. You can omit pertinent details or leave out necessary information and feel as though you didn't actually tell a lie. In doing this, you may think you were honest in a situation. But it is up to us to be guided by integrity no matter what it costs us in the moment. Honesty will always bring about the best results.

Is there an area of your life where you are struggling with honesty? It is a trap of the enemy to keep you thinking that there is absolutely no way out of that situation without utter ruin. I promise that the way out is through truth. You can never be truly free without being completely honest. Decide today to live free!

<u>Day 13</u>

Whew! Thank the Lord that He didn't come back to get us today because there ain't no way He would have recognized me after I just spent all day in a chlorine swimming pool. Note to self: That's probably a sure-fire way to get left behind!

Heaven

Acts 1:11 *(NIV) – "Men of Galilee," they said, "why do you stand here looking into the sky? This same Jesus, who has been taken from you into heaven, will come back in the same way you have seen him go into heaven."*

I can't believe that I am headed out the door to Wal-Mart at almost 11 p.m.! I forgot to pick up makeup remover cloths and I can't take waking up again tomorrow with my eyes glued shut from this waterproof mascara. It really gave me quite a scare this morning when I went to open my eyes, and they didn't! It took me a few seconds to realize that I had not died. Even if I had, I quickly deduced that surely there would be a better thread count on sheets in heaven than the ones I was currently laying on.

So many people have questions concerning our afterlife. Whether you agree on how or when or any of the other specifics concerning what we refer to as the rapture, there is a way to be completely sure of where you will spend eternity. Whether you have a specific belief concerning this event or you are the person with several questions, one thing is for sure; allowing Jesus to become Lord of your life is definitely the way in which you will live forever.

If you are unsure of where you will spend eternity, I encourage you to make the best decision of your life by surrendering it to Christ. There is no peace on earth like knowing that death is not our final end. You and I can live eternally with the One who created us.

<u>*Day 14*</u>

There are only a handful of women that you should trust completely: your mom, your sister, your best friend, and Little Debbie!

Trust

Proverbs 3:5 *(NIV) - Trust in the LORD with all your heart and lean not on your own understanding;*

While shopping in a new store through displays of clothing that could only be described as the Daisy Duke Spring Collection, I was approached by a sales girl who asked if I needed any assistance. I was so relieved. I thanked her and quietly asked to see the "more forgiving" sized clothing. She smiled and very discreetly showed me the way to a more suitable section. I could tell that this particular store did not have many women shop in my section due to it being unmarked and all the way in the back. I mean, we had to weave in and out of racks, through aisles, and across hallways together. Seriously, Sacajawea must have had an easier time guiding Lewis and Clark to the West! Anyway, when my guide offered to make a few selections for me and bring them to the dressing room, I eagerly agreed. I made myself comfortable inside the dressing room stall and waited for my personal shopper to return. Within just a few minutes, she returned carrying several trendy items. (I should note here that when a sales girl asks you to promise her that you will at least try everything on, it may be a precursor of things to come.) Even sitting here today, I am unsure how the intoxicating sounds of her chanting, "Awww, trust me, that is so super cute on you!" after each outfit, led me to not only believe her, but also purchase a sweater, that after I put it on, it looked like it should snap between the legs and have OshKosh printed on the tag!

Trust is something that can be so hard to give and so easy to loose. When we put our complete confidence in others there will be times that, in their humanness, they will mishandle that confidence. God instructs us to put our complete trust in Him. He is fully capable of handling our trust with the greatest of care.

Today, put your trust in the One who will never let you down, the One who can not lie, and the One whose very words are the complete truth for your life!

Day 15

My neighbor's dog has been barking for an hour. I'm about to go do the Christian thing and baptize it... with a water hose!

Kindness

Ephesians 4:32 *(NIV) – Be kind and compassionate to one another, forgiving each other, just as in Christ God forgave you.*

It is an understatement to say that I have recently been experiencing slight mood swings. I am trying to eliminate any reason that could cause me to unnecessarily bite people's heads off. With that being said, I moved my appointment to check my hormone levels up by a few weeks. I am hoping that this is indeed the issue. If not, my family's theory of why I have been in a bad mood for six months just got blown out of the water, as well as, my theory for why I would like to hold them all under water!

It can certainly be a challenge to show kindness sometimes. Whether it is because you just don't want to or whether you believe that you have every reason not to, there will never be a good excuse to be unkind. Not only does Christ command us to be kind and compassionate to each other, but He also reminds us of how kind He has been to us when we deserved nothing at all.

Go through this day determined to show kindness to someone. Whether it is deserved or not is not the requirement, only your willingness to show genuine kindness and love just as Christ has shown you.

Day 16

Dear Terrible Twos,

I would like to apologize for cursing you as the worst houseguest that I would ever have years ago. I have recently met your smarty pants older brother and I must say, that if you are ever this way again and would like to swap out a visit with him, you are welcomed.

Sincerely,
The Mom Of A Teenager

Parenting

Proverbs 22:6 (NIV) - Start children off on the way they should go, and even when they are old they will not turn from it.

I will never forget bringing each of my sons to my chest immediately after their birth and being overwhelmed by my immediate love for them. I remember staring into their little faces while thinking, "I wonder if they will ever know how blessed I feel to be their mom?" Fast forward to twelve and seventeen years later. I am now staring up at my bathrobe hanging on the back of a door, drowning out a voice on the other side while thinking, "I wonder if they will ever know that I just want to be left alone while I'm in the bathroom?" Seriously, I do want to be a great mom. But even after all of these years, I have yet to perfect even a piece of it. Being a great mom is the Rubik's cube of my life. No matter how much I practice, I really just want to take the colored stickers off and cheat!

I love that God foreknew we would sometimes experience a lack of confidence in our own ability as parents. He promised us in His word that if we would just teach them and train them, He would make it happen. No matter what seasons we find ourselves in with our children, God promises that they will walk in His truths that we have taught them.

Know today that despite the season or situation surrounding your children, they were the Lord's before they were yours and He will be faithful to His word!

Day 17

I am past needing a pedicure. I may have to call a blacksmith.

Appearance

1 Peter 3:3 (NIV) - Your beauty should not come from outward adornment, such as elaborate hairstyles and the wearing of gold jewelry or fine clothes.

After today, I am quite certain that the same person who invented barbed wire also invented underwire! It's just been one of those days. First of all, while coloring my own hair, I decide to read all the fine print on the box which read: "May not cover all grays in order to produce a highlighted effect." Really? My translation is that this hair color does not work. Then I went to have my eyebrows waxed and the new girl lost her grip when pulling off the tape...TWICE! Now my eyelids are glowing bright red. Each time that I blink, it looks like someone is shooting off flares in my living room.

I often have to remind myself that real beauty does not come from the way that I look. Real beauty comes from the inward part of me; the part that is loving, honest, and peaceful. We live in a world that glorifies outward beauty and dismisses anything that doesn't fit into its definition of what is beautiful. As women, we have to continuously remind ourselves that who we are on the inside far exceeds what we may look like on the outside.

Take a moment to find a mirror and look directly at your reflection. Not around it, but directly at it. Remind yourself that you are more than just the features that you see staring back at you. If you haven't heard it in a while, let me just say, "You are beautiful!"

Day 18

Although money isn't the key to happiness, I'm sure with enough of it, you could get a key made!

Prosperity

Job 36:11 *(NIV) - If they obey and serve him, they will spend the rest of their days in prosperity and their years in contentment.*

I have found that money will not bring happiness. It will only bring things like cars, houses, shoes and jewelry. (This has also led me to believe that happiness may be overrated!) I don't know at what age you realize your family's financial status but for me it was around the time that my younger brother was in elementary school and had a friend over for dinner. My mother wasn't feeling well and went to her room to rest awhile. After dinner my brother was helping rinse the dishes when I heard his guest ask, "Where is your dishwasher?" to which my brother replied, "Oh, she went to lay down." I remember thinking that I knew what a dishwasher was from seeing one at my girlfriend's house during a slumber party, but my brother had no clue. I quickly told his friend that we had to put ours in the shop!

God most certainly wants us to be prosperous and without lack. Prosperity means increase in every area of our lives (family, ministry, career, finances, health, marriage, parenting, etc.). Poverty in any area is not His will for us. His word is very clear on this principle. He is also clear on how we should steward that prosperity when it is in the form of finances. To show obedience with our money shows God that money does not control us. Money is nothing more than a tool that takes on the power or intention of the one using it. Money is neither inheritably good nor evil...it is the LOVE of money that we are warned will destroy us. Money in the hands of the right person can be a long awaited answer to another person. That is what it means to say that we are blessed to be a blessing!

Make up your mind today that God most certainly wants you to experience prosperity and that you will not settle for lack in ANY area of your life!

Day 19

I do not eat birthday cake, not just because of the way it taste (yuck!) but because there is no other food that I purposely eat after someone has lit it on fire and then blew spit all over it.

<u>Aging</u>

Psalm 91:16 *(NIV) - With long life I will satisfy him and show him my salvation.*

SIX MINUTES!!! I stood in the Kroger parking lot for six whole minutes while I thought to myself, "Now Lisa, c'mon you can do this. Where would you be if you were a green Toyota?" All I could think of was how just days before I started to buy some vitamins that claimed to support memory health but decided that I was much too young for such a purchase. But how right now, I would tear the cap off the bottle with my teeth and inhale a handful of them if I thought that they would help me find my car. Since I couldn't seem to locate it in a reasonable amount of time and since people had begun to stare, I did what any self-respecting woman of almost forty years of age would do. I curbed my cart full of groceries and pretended to take an unexpected call on my cell phone as I also continued scanning the parking lot for my car!

God is the giver of life. His desire for you and me is to live a long fruitful one. Although society sometimes paints an unflattering picture of aging, we know that the alternative is worse. To not age means to not be here and, yes, that is absolutely worse. The reality is that age accompanies the most beautiful things that this life has to offer. No one has the privilege of appreciating endless true love, a lifelong best friend, or an adoring grandchild without the gift of aging.

Decide today to embrace your age. Live whatever number that you happen to be with great appreciation. You haven't seen anything yet. Your best is yet to come!

<u>Day 20</u>

I'm not really a woman who could be described as a "trophy wife." Honestly, I feel more like a "yellow-state-fair-ribbon-for-honorable-mention" kind of wife.

Marriage

Genesis 2:18 *(NIV) - The LORD God said, It is not good for the man to be alone. I will make a helper suitable for him.*

Having known my husband since seventh grade and having been married to him for fifteen years now, it is clear to me that God has a serious funny bone. I mentally picture my marriage as God's own, personal sitcom. I am also certain he is very excited about DVR, because surely even God fast forwards through commercials. Commercials are what I like to call the stormy seasons of my marriage. I am very grateful for having them because they have definitely *sponsored* the rest of our show; however, no one really wants to sit through them over and over. You know, like the time we were in marriage counseling or years before that, when our one year old son was in our wedding. (Trivia side note here: It is frowned upon to list a "virgin birth" as experience on a Christian college transcript. It will not be considered as extra credit.)

God knew that Richie and I would endure many things, some of which statistics predicted would hinder us from getting married altogether or ultimately would lead us to a divorce. However, statistics did not consider that the God of the universe put in us every single thing that we would need to overcome and triumph, no matter what! The same is true for you and your husband. No matter what you may be facing in your marriage, just remember, with God all things are possible!

Today, know that God's greatest desire for your marriage is wholeness. Whatever needs mending, improving, weathering, or just plain celebrating, he has equipped you to do it.

Day 21

While flipping through a friend's photo album, I asked if a particular picture was someone related to her because they sort of resembled one another. She replied, "Ummm, no. That was me before I had the kids."

Criticism

Proverbs 3:5 *(NIV) - The words of the reckless pierce like swords, but the tongue of the wise brings healing.*

I recently left my house in a hurry without really styling my hair. I am sure that you can guess what I heard over and over, all day. I don't think I saw one person who didn't ask, "Did you get your hair cut?" I am not fond of how we use this secret code to advise another woman that her hair looks a mess. I just really wanted to say, "No, I didn't get a hair cut, but while we are asking questions, are you retaining water?"

Somehow we manage to criticize other people so easily. (I actually believe that this has a lot to do with our own insecurities.) If we really understood that we have the power to bring healing and confidence to someone's life, I am sure that we would do that more freely. Words are powerful and the ones that we choose to use can lift others up or tear them down. I must admit, it does seem more difficult for women to gain control of this area. We are much more vocal and open than most men. But we are not left without help. The Lord promises that we can do ALL things through Him. And yes, that even means gaining control of our mouths!

Purpose in your heart today that you will not be reckless and cutting with your words; that you will instead be wise and use them to bring healing and life to someone else!

Day 22

I slept like a rock last night! It's probably because I recently started taking every big girl's least favorite sleep aid…exercise.

Rest

Matthew 11:28 (NIV) - Come to me, all you who are weary and burdened, and I will give you rest.

It amazes me how much is on my to-do list at the beginning of every week. You know that you have had a busy schedule when you slip an allergy pill into your kids' breakfast cereal because you can't remember the last time that you did any dusting or vacuuming. I race to get all of the things on my list accomplished by the end of the week and still sometimes I fall short. For years, when I worked outside the home, it was much worse. Back then some things just got neglected all together. I mean who really needs a dentist appointment? (We brush and floss everyday, right?) And I dare say that no one has actually died of embarrassment (despite what my boys may have said happened to that one kid in gym class) from wearing mismatched socks to school when the laundry is piled high.

In the busyness of life, we tend to forget that so much of what we are going through is just for a season. Our children grow up, our careers change, our marriages mature, and so on, and so on. Most of these periods of overwhelming busyness will not last forever; they are just seasons of our lives. During these seasons it is important to find rest. You are no good to anyone, including yourself, if you don't take the time to rest.

Carve out some time this week to rest. Give the Lord whatever is weighing you down, consuming your time, and adding stress to your days. He can handle it and has promised an awesome exchange for each of these things.

Day 23

The fair is in town! It's an entire week of great food, cool prizes, and getting together with family. It's like Hanukkah for the trailer park.

Home

Proverbs 15:16 *(NIV) - Better a little with the fear of the L*ORD *than great wealth with turmoil.*

I heard about a couple in Salt Lake City who set up a camera to record their neighbor who dressed in a disguise and broke into their home using a key that they had once given her. She stole thousands of dollars in cash from their home on several different occasions. Now, where I came from this would never happen. Why? Because in the trailer park we didn't have video equipment...that happened to be ours, at least. If any one of the park's thirty-eight dogs began to bark, we would all look out from behind our bed sheet curtains to see if it was our dog and who was in our yard. If we saw anyone acting strange and dressing in a disguise, we knew someone was trying to hide from either a parole officer or child support, so we would just call both. We watched everyone's trailer, whether asked to or not, and if you weren't supposed to be on the porch, we called the law. If you were using a key, we knew that you were not supposed to be there, because we didn't even use the key. You were not going to find thousands of dollars in our homes just lying around, unless of course, you caught us at tax time. And you sure weren't going to find it on several occasions! (Unless you count that guy who lived in lot #17 and claimed that all his money came from his "internet business.")

I value the sense of belonging that I have when I am surrounded by family and those closest to me. Many times this feeling occurs when I happen to be where I live and other times this feeling occurs when I am in the midst of a community. In this day and age, what we consider "home" varies greatly. Whether it's a dwelling or a community of people, I have come to realize that when you have the sanctity of somewhere to call home, you are truly blessed.

Many would love to have what we so easily take for granted. Decide today that you will be grateful for the home that God has blessed you with. Whether in a shack, apartment, trailer, house, mansion, or just right in the middle of those who value you the most, your "home" is indeed blessed.

<u>*Day 24*</u>

Is it too much to expect not to have bad breath if you just drank peppermint flavored coffee? Shouldn't they cancel each other out?

Expectation

Hebrews 10:35 *(NIV) - So do not throw away your confidence; it will be richly rewarded.*

I was recently asked: "What is your most comfortable piece of clothing?" My reply: "Maternity underwear." Next question followed: "Oh, are you expecting?" My response: "Yes, I am expecting him to have his room cleaned before I get back home. He's in middle school." As a mother, expectation tends to be my greatest "frienemy." Some days we are the best of pals and then other days, we just want to key each other's car!

Expectation is tricky like that, sometimes we hope for and expect the very best and things just don't turn out. Maybe we're expecting something unrealistic or something that was not yet time or maybe, just maybe, we had every right to expect something and someone let us down. Either way, we grow from it. There will never be a good enough reason to stop having great expectation!

God reminds us in His word that our expectation will be richly rewarded. We do not get to qualify what that reward will be but rest assured if it is from God, it is exactly what is needed to bring blessing to our life.

Decide today that you will expect the very best of whatever situation you are facing. It will be in that expectation that you will find your reward.

Day 25

Yesterday, I finally cashed in a long awaited upgrade in order to get a new smartphone. I felt really smart lying in bed last night as I stared at the ceiling too afraid to fall asleep because I couldn't find the alarm clock setting on this thing.

Patience

Ecclesiastes 7:8 *(NIV) - The end of a matter is better than its beginning, and patience is better than pride.*

Okay, so I was in between hair appointments and couldn't wait any longer to get my hair colored. I decided to have my sister help me out before my next comedy engagement and just until I could get to the hairdresser. (I am known to do this from time to time when I can't wait for an available appointment.) My sister has always done most of my family's hair so I had no concerns at all about her coloring mine. However, had I known that she had decided to leave red hair color on my head for twice the allotted time allowed, I would have expressed some concern! She explained that the box advised to "leave on longer for stubborn grays" and she further explained that mine not only seemed stubborn, but also rebellious and needed a longer time to process. Needless to say that when I arrived at my upcoming comedy engagement, they were surprised to see that they had somehow booked a postpartum version of Peppermint Patty!

Patience is an area that most people struggle with daily. I seem to struggle with it minute by minute! However, when I take the time to wait, I find that things generally turn out much better than if I'd rushed into something. Time isn't motivated by anything that we have or could offer. Time will pass whether we are here to witness it or not. Whether it is awaiting an unanswered prayer or strength to keep going in a season; if you are patient, your waiting will produce your help.

For every moment that you find yourself wanting to rush through or hurry over a moment, take just another moment to remind yourself that you are not capable of knowing all that God knows. Waiting is part of His process for our lives and it develops many valuable things within us. He created time and knows best how to use it in our life. Trust Him as you wait.

<u>*Day 26*</u>

Dear Jesus, please help me to resist all of the half-priced chocolate that I will encounter after this holiday is over. Strengthen me now to only crave fruit or at the very least, Raisinettes. Amen.

Overcoming

1 John 4:4 *(NIV) - You, dear children, are from God and have overcome them, because the one who is in you is greater than the one who is in the world.*

In light of all the negative information that we often see on the nightly news, I really love a good human interest story. Last night I watched an inspiring story of a baseball player who got back up to bat after getting hit in the head last season by a ninety-two-mile-an- hour pitch. I like to think that I am resilient, but I just really don't know if I could've done it. Seriously, back in 2008 I got a bug caught in my hair while driving twenty-five miles an hour through a school zone and I haven't had my windows down since!

It takes more than just courage to overcome. It also requires trust. The only courage that you need is the courage to trust an unseen God who lives in your heart and is completely capable of handling anything that you may be facing today. When we put our trust in Him, the pressure to overcome is suddenly off of our shoulders. There is no need to wonder whether or not you have it in you to overcome. If He is in you, then you can rest assure that you have all you need!

Make up your mind to trust whole heartedly that greater is the One who lives in you than the one who lives in the world!

<u>Day 27</u>

As my oldest son was reading aloud an article from his science textbook, I hear him say, "Mom did you fall asleep?" I replied, "Uh, no sweetie, I was praying for God to expand your mind and help you." He asked, "Then why were you snoring?" "Well, honey, I was trying to get God's attention."

Prayer

Colossians 4:2 *(NIV) - Devote yourselves to prayer, being watchful and thankful.*

This morning, I took Benadryl for my allergy which is making me drowsy and Afrin for my sinuses, which is making me hyper. So all morning right in the middle of talking ninety miles an hour, I occasionally pass out for a quick twelve-second nap! To play it off, I just acted like I was praying. On another note, I'd like to give God praise for allowing me to hold an altar call in the Sonic drive-thru with the concerned people that had gathered as I "napped" in the middle of placing my Dr. Pepper order. Apparently, ordering a "Doctor" in the drive-thru speaker just before passing out, gets people's attention. Who knew? Anyway, we had one saved, two rededications and a very large tater tot offering!

I remember many years ago I thought prayer had to be some eloquently spoken speech presented to God in a language that sounded like my bible. Over the years, I have come to know that prayer is simply talking to God and spending time with Him just like you would your best friend. It is how we develop a really genuine relationship with Him. No worthwhile relationship was ever built without the key ingredient of time. Prayer can be done anywhere, anytime, and anyway. The more personal, the more true to your style, the better!

Determine that you will spend some time with the Lord today. He longs to spend time with you each day. Just like spending time talking with anyone else, the more that you do it, the more comfortable it becomes. If you don't know where to start, begin by thanking Him for all that you have!

Day 28

As a married woman, I have often wondered if love is blind then why is lingerie so popular?

<u>*Love*</u>

1 Corinthians 13:4 (NIV) - Love is patient, love is kind. It does not envy, it does not boast, it is not proud.

I was having coffee with a friend when she confided that she was giving up on online dating after trying it for only a short time. I advised her to grab a clothespin and hang on to that line! I mean, we aren't getting any younger you know. And let me just say that there is nothing wrong with being single, if that is what you want. However, if you want to be in a relationship and eventually in a marriage, well you're going to have to hang in there a little while. You can't just give up. I explained that we live in an information age where online dating is now the preferred way to meet and mingle. The last time I checked, dating takes two people and the way that I do math meant she was halfway there. Although I have never personally experienced it, I would guess that online dating is very similar to online shopping. I did warn her to be careful because like anything else online, I'm sure the shipping and handling is where they really get you.

I don't know of any woman who, as a teenager, did not desire to fall madly in love with the man of her dreams someday. And while many women still feel this way, they have cut themselves off from any possible interaction with men because of the ones that have hurt them in the past. Don't misunderstand me; I absolutely do not believe in casual dating. However, you can not fall madly in love with someone without at least asking their first name. At some point you will have to take a chance and trust someone in order to find love.

Begin to seek God concerning any unforgiveness or bitterness that you may need to release from past relationships. Decide today that you will trust the Lord's timing as He reveals that person made just for you!

Day 29

From the kitchen, I hear, "Mom, I think I'm abducted!" I ask, "How can you tell?" He explains, "I can't quit eating these oranges!" My response, "Oh, well you may be addicted, but I feel certain that you are not abducted." As I hear him trail off in a whisper, "If you say so."

Wisdom

Proverbs 4:7 *(NIV) - The beginning of wisdom is this: Get wisdom. Though it cost all you have, get understanding.*

Being a home school mom has its challenges. When I first began home schooling my sons, they were in the third and seventh grade. I quickly realized two things: My youngest son believed I was a direct descendant of Albert Einstein and my oldest son seemed to wonder how I had ever mastered the art of tying my own shoes. Having attended some college and worked with children during my professional career, and just plain being a mom, led me to think, how hard could this be? I remember our first week in math. My youngest son had equations like, "If Johnny has six apples and Mary has four apples, how many apples do they have together?" After reading the question, I replied, "Ten apples!" To which my son shouts, "Good job, mom!" But my oldest son had much more complicated equations. Ones that read, "If Johnny has six apples, takes a bite of each one of them, places all of his apples in Mary's basket, then she gets on a train traveling at one hundred miles per hour toward the sun, and decides to eat one of those apples for lunch, what does she have?" Surprised that I actually knew the answer, I shouted, "Mono! And that's why we don't eat after people. Next question, please."

I have learned that knowledge is nothing but information. It is wisdom that knows what to do with that information. God's word declares that just the act of seeking wisdom means that you are wise! He has promised us that He will give it to us liberally, if we seek Him for it. What a promise!

Decide today to seek the wisdom and understanding of the Lord for your own life through His word. He assures us that we will find it!

Day 30

A good, hearty laugh relieves physical tension and stress, leaving your muscles relaxed for up to 45 minutes afterwards. So there you have it; my muscles are not untoned, they are just relaxed!

Laughter

Proverbs 17:22 *(NIV) - A cheerful heart is good medicine, but a crushed spirit dries up the bones.*

I remember being a young teenager sitting in church one Sunday as I watched my older sister file into the choir loft to sing with the other members. Just before this, she and I had been in the ladies room discussing my poor attitude about not being old enough to join the choir and how I would feel better if I just smiled or maybe even laughed. Sitting in my pew sulking, I watched my sister come out of the side choir entrance, face first and smiling. As she turned and started making her way up the small choir aisle to take her seat up on the back row, I couldn't help but be filled with a smile myself. Apparently she was in such a hurry to leave the ladies room that she neglected to check the back of her dress which was now tucked right into the back of her pantyhose. Well, one thing is for sure, she was right. I certainly did feel a lot better after I started to laugh!

Have you ever had to battle a bad attitude, been really disappointed, or even just sad? Sure, we all have. And, yes, sometimes it is even while in church. However, the greatest weapon in my arsenal has always been laughter. I have yet to come up against anything that, given enough time, laughter could not help. It instantly makes you feel better and even gives you a few moments to forget whatever may be weighing you down.

Determine today that you will find some laughter, regardless of your situation. You may have to look harder than anyone else but, I promise, it is there. When you find it, take a big dose and soak up all the benefits that it is sure to bring!

Day 31

I'm not really as much of an "out-of-the-box" thinker as I am a "set-the-box-on-fire-and-draw-a-crowd" kind of girl!

Purpose

Exodus 9:16 *(NIV) – But I have raised you up for this very purpose, that I might show you my power and that my name might be proclaimed in all the earth.*

I am definitely not the quiet type. When I have a preference or a belief that needs to be hailed from the rooftops, I don't have a problem making that happen. For years I wondered how growing up very shy around others led to such openness as an adult. I remember being terrified of bringing any attention to myself at school. But at home, somehow the sanctity of a single wide trailer offered a stage that allowed me the freedom to juggle our cat and a set of steak knives if I thought it could bring a laugh to my family. A couple of times I even tried to make my brothers "disappear." (At the time of this writing, my sisters-in-law have started a fund in order to further my magician training.) I also wasn't the smartest family clown. In an effort to make my sister laugh one night before bed, I bet her that I could kick my leg higher than she could. I held my arm straight out in front of me, planted my back leg firmly and then swung my other leg up to touch my hand. Had I calculated the width of that Strawberry Shortcake nightgown better, you might be talking to the next Mary Lou Retton! Sadly, geometry wasn't my strong suit even back then. After I kicked my leg, my nightgown swept the other leg right out from under me, dropping me to the floor and almost knocking me unconscious! (My sister is still laughing to this day.)

The passion to make others laugh was imprinted into my spirit long before I understood why. God knew that one day I would use comedy to point people toward His great love. He knew it because He put it there. I know with certainty that your passion is directly related to your purpose! If you are unsure of what that could be, seek the Lord for it. He absolutely will not withhold it from you. It is His desire that you walk it out with great power!

Decide today that nothing will keep you from living a life of passionate purpose!

Testimonial

Being that I meet many people under the pretense of comedy, there is sort of a misconception about my life. Because I am full of personality and ready to share humor at any given moment, most people just assume that I have always been a very happy person. In actuality, this couldn't be further from the truth. To help you to understand why I am so grateful to live a life filled with joy now and why I am so very passionate about helping others find joy as well, I'll share a little about my past. So in the spirit of understanding and as an opportunity to give glory to God, here we go!

I had my first nervous breakdown when I was seven years old. I remained under treatment until I was nine, but would eventually relapse into three more breakdowns before the age of thirty. The first one was scarier for my mother than for me. I really had no concept of what was going on around me as I went through all kinds of tests to conclude that there was absolutely no medical reason why my esophagus should be collapsing. I tried to get a handle on what the older folk around me kept calling "bad nerves." As a teenager and young adult, I tried very hard to battle several long seasons of depression only to have them result in other breakdowns.

As a child, no one really knew how anxious I was or how much I worried. I did not know that was what I was doing. Actually, I didn't know that I was doing anything. I never had a name for it or even knew that it was an "it." To me worrying was just the way that I thought and anxiety was the way that I felt. The fear that surrounded my young life, when put into the computer of my brain came out as worry. By the same token, the constant state of that fear became anxiety. I talked to several adults. I answered many questions. I learned all kinds of ways to think more positive, but I could never figure out what the big deal was. These two things were as much a part of me as my arms and legs. I could not just make them stop nor did I want to. This was my first taste of what control felt like. I could not change the things in my environment that would cause me to be gripped with fear but I could obsess about them. I could not make them go away, but I could try to steer them. Worry and anxiety are not things felt by young children to gain attention. Manifesting real physical ailments was not a trick that I had learned or picked up. As a matter of fact, I would often try to hide it in an attempt to shield my family, who had a front row seat, watching me struggle with what we now know was the onset of severe anxiety and depression.

In some bizarre way, through all of that, I learned to cope with life through humor. I became the family clown as a way to self medicate. Laughter and tears became my closest allies. As I got older, I learned through trial and error that cycles of medications and seasons of counseling were not going to fix what was broken in my life. Despite seeing others have success with various forms of treatments; I decided to take matters into my own hands in order to ensure the best defense. I tried to self medicate through other avenues, including relationships, work, alcohol, and later on, even ministry. When none of them worked, I came to the conclusion that there was little hope for me.

It wasn't until I had a life changing experience with God that I became aware of His unimaginable love that held the power to heal. My husband and I were having marital problems. In fact, we even separated and filed for divorce. My children were both having medical issues that were draining our family emotionally. Our car was being repossessed, and we were being evicted from our home. During this time, my depression and anxiety were out of control. Needless to say, all was not well on the home front when God decided that He and I would get down to business about this whole "religion" thing. You see, years earlier, I had been miserable as a party girl and now I was just as miserable as a ministry leader. I didn't realize that all I had done was change locations and that is simply just geography. I needed to be changed, I needed to be delivered, and there was only one way to do it. I cried out to God. I had always believed that He had saved me from hell, but I now needed Him to save me from myself.

He was so faithful! By surrendering what I thought I knew of Him and how I thought He wanted me to act and live, I gained a new life of amazing love and incredible freedom. It was like an etch-a-sketch. My whole life was shaken vigorously only to be left with a clean slate. I left all of the "religiousness" behind and began developing a relationship with God that was based only on the honesty of His heart and mine. It was through this process that I began to experience emotional and mental healing that I had never known. I can honestly say that I have never been as fulfilled in Christ as I am today. He picked up all of those broken pieces of my life and fashioned them together in a beautiful mosaic of His mercy and grace. He breathed healing to my mind, love to my heart, and life to my spirit.

I walk in a purpose that is clear and in a confidence that could only come from Him. It is such an honor to be given the opportunity to stand on stage and use comedy to point others to the love of Christ. I am blessed to share His truth. The truth that happiness is temporary and based on your circumstances but joy is within you and it is forever. The bible declares in the book of Nehemiah that the joy of the Lord is our strength. I truly believe that this strength is what enables us to live a powerful life of purpose. As a little girl, I may not have understood the reason, but I did know that there was healing in laughter.

Reflection

I don't know what the formula is that makes a perfect joke. Some say it's content. Others say it's delivery. However, my favorite theory is timing. I laugh the loudest and longest when something has been filtered through "perfect timing." I believe that when timing is the focus of anything, it meets the need at the most perfect place. Life is the same way. I have learned that timing is a crucial element that is most often over looked and extremely underestimated.

What you hold in your hand is a direct result of the timing of God. Many times I have tried to pen pages that I thought would bring laughter, give inspiration or speak life. However, the Lord has waited until now to release me to do it. Not knowing the fullness of His reasoning, I can only speculate that He has strategically waited until now so that it would meet a need at the most perfect place.

It has certainly been an honor to have shared this collection of thoughts and devotions with you. I want you to know that I prayed for you long before you purchased or even creased the binding of this book. I thought about you as I wrote and as I laughed aloud. I pictured your face and asked God to love on you through these pages in a way that you would know could only come from Him. Through this book, I pray that you have experienced some time with the Lord that may be different than what you normally experience. Maybe you laughed a little. Maybe you related some. Maybe you even prayed differently a couple of times. My hope is that you have come to know that Christ desires a real relationship with you. Not one that is coated in deep doctrine, religious rhetoric, church chatter, or even your best behavior. All He desires is a relationship that is filled with your complete self, authentically given back to Him as an offering of love.

If you would like to begin a relationship like that with Him and make Jesus the Lord of your life, you can do that right where you are. You do not have to be inside of a church. You do not have to get on your knees. As a matter of fact, you don't even have to close your eyes. Just simply say...

"Jesus, I surrender myself to You. I ask that You come into my life, forgive me, and make me whole with the inward knowledge of who You are and who You created me to be. I believe that You died on a cross to save me and then You rose from the grave so that I could live eternally with You. Thank You for loving me. You are mine and I am Yours, forever. Amen"

If you prayed that prayer, I invite you to contact me at lisamillslol@gmail.com so that I may rejoice with you in celebrating the greatest decision of your life!

Acknowledgements

I believe that you know more about a person by knowing whom they honor than any other piece of information that they could reveal about themselves. Although you don't normally see many "thank you" pages rounding out a collection of devotions, I have decided that there are several people in my life that MORE than deserve to be honored publicly so I would like to take this opportunity to do it right here.

Disclaimer: *If your name is not mentioned here, this probably will not interest you. Therefore if you have ADD, feel free to skip to the end of the book if you need to. However, if you have OCD and absolutely will not be able to sleep without reading this book in the order in which it was written, then continue to the next paragraph. And lastly, even if you do not care about nor know any of these people but have a severe case of NOSEY then absolutely continue reading. Hopefully this part will interest you as well.*

First, I would like to acknowledge my Lord, Jesus Christ, who since before time began had a plan for my life. He came to this earth and gave His life for me to be able to live mine with great power and freedom. Christ is not the most important thing IN my life...He IS my life.

I would like to publicly thank my husband, Richie, for saving me the only way that a man can save a woman, by loving her more than he loves himself. Thank you for always believing in my dreams, for being my very best friend, and for demonstrating your complete loyalty to our commitment, time and time again. I am so grateful to walk along this journey side by side with you. I love you more than this lifetime will ever allow me to express.

Thank you to my amazing sons. Despite all the joke-writing sessions they have always taken the call on my life seriously. Both of you give me the grace to get up each day and try to work this "Mom" thing out. All while you reassure me that I am doing a terrific job. (Between us three, we all know that "terrific" is probably not very accurate.) Thank you for always allowing me the freedom to reach outside of my role as your mother in order to passionately share what God has branded onto my heart. Know that absolutely nothing that I have done or will ever do could top being your mom. It excites me to know that your purposes, callings, and dreams are greater than anything I have ever known. You two are my greatest blessings; I love you both with my whole heart.

To my pastor and spiritual father, Bishop Jeff Poole, I would like to say that my life would not be what it is today without your ministry. Your belief in me means more to me than you could ever know. Hardly a week has gone by over the last fifteen years that I have not thanked God that you were obedient to the call. Where I had always believed that I was born to fight, you made me believe that I was born to win! Your life has forever changed mine. For that I am so grateful. I love you dearly, sir.

Thank you to my spiritual mother, Denise Smith, for loving me on purpose and becoming one of the greatest treasures of my life. You came along at a time when I was hurt the most. You brought with you healing that would redirect the course of my life forever. You taught me that love is the most important thing and that significance far outweighs success. I am so grateful for your presence in my life. My heart is melted to yours in a way that only a daughter's could be, forever and always. I love you very much.

To one of my dearest friends and also my personal life coach, Pastor Jonas Alday, I can honestly say that I would not be doing what I am today without your coaching. Fifteen years ago, you eagerly recruited me onto a team. You helped me learn to read a playbook of success. Then, you stood on the sidelines for all of those years coaching through every fumble, strategizing through every play, and celebrating through every touchdown. Long before there was ever the dream of Lisa Out Loud, there was just Lisa with a lot of obstacles and opponents. One by one, with you coaching me, I overcame every one of them to pursue a different kind of life. You have helped me turn the impossible into the incredible! From the bottom of my heart and with so much love and respect I want to say, thank you for never giving up on me.

To Dawn Alday, thank you just doesn't seem good enough. Your friendship is one of my greatest blessings. There are no words to describe what your life has meant to mine. I honestly know that I would have quit a long time ago had it not been for your encouragement. Before I learned the scriptures, it was your life that I had begun to read. You were the woman of God who mentored, coached, listened, prayed, laughed, cried, and celebrated with me before anyone else did and long after others stopped. You reached back, held on tight, and refused to leave me behind. I have never known a more authentic woman who loves God with all of her heart than you. Know that today, I honor and love you with all of my heart. Proverbs 31:30, "Charm is deceptive, and beauty is fleeting; but a woman who fears the Lord is to be praised."

Also, thank you to an amazing woman, my Aunt Geneva Bussell. For many years you traveled back and forth up Hwy 247 to make sure that my family had an opportunity to see Christ's love in action. Even as a child, I knew that what you had was the real deal. The love I felt around you was a testament to the love that I would come to know years later from Christ. Thank you for all of your sacrifice and for every seed that you sowed into my life.

Lastly, but certainly not least, to the woman who volunteered during an Awana program for kids in Macon, Georgia thirty something years ago, thank you for introducing me to a beautiful Savior. Although I never knew your name, I can still clearly see your smile. Because you volunteered your time in ministry on a random Wednesday night, I was able to hear how a Man loved me so much that He died to save me. You presented the gospel to me with such love, His love. With tears flowing down my little cheeks, and a warm feeling that I didn't understand, I prayed to make Him Lord over my life. My life forever changed in that one moment. Thank you.

Information

Lisa Mills is often invited to share her testimony and stand up comedy with audiences across the nation. If you would like to invite her to fellowship with your organization through comedy, inspirational or testimonial speaking, please feel free to contact her through www.lisaoutloud.net

Lisa Mills supports all of the following: Clean water projects in Africa, Christian based counseling centers in the U.S., and diabetes awareness throughout the Middle Georgia community. If you would like more information regarding these efforts, how you can support these causes, or the overall ministry of Lisa Out Loud, please visit www.lisaoutloud.net

Lisa is proud to be a part of a diversely, thriving body of believers at New Hope International Church where she has served faithfully in ministry for the past fifteen years under the leadership of Bishop Jeff and Pastor Lisa Poole. It has been through this ministry and the personal life coaching from Pastor Jonas Alday of Dreams Work Coaching, which have led Lisa to discover a very simple, yet profound truth: The beauty of your most authentic self is revealed only when you take your rightful place on the path to your purpose!

You may also find out more about New Hope International and Dreams Work Coaching and Consulting through:

www.lisaoutloud.net